Animal Classes

Amphibians

by Julie Murray

Dash!
LEVELED READERS
An Imprint of Abdo Zoom • abdopublishing.com

Dash!
LEVELED READERS

Level 1 – Beginning
Short and simple sentences with familiar words or patterns for children who are beginning to understand how letters and sounds go together.

Level 2 – Emerging
Longer words and sentences with more complex language patterns for readers who are practicing common words and letter sounds.

Level 3 – Transitional
More developed language and vocabulary for readers who are becoming more independent.

abdopublishing.com

Published by Abdo Zoom, a division of ABDO, PO Box 398166, Minneapolis, Minnesota 55439.
Copyright © 2019 by Abdo Consulting Group, Inc. International copyrights reserved in all countries.
No part of this book may be reproduced in any form without written permission from the publisher.
Dash!™ is a trademark and logo of Abdo Zoom.

Printed in the United States of America, North Mankato, Minnesota.
052018
092018

Photo Credits: iStock, Shutterstock
Production Contributors: Kenny Abdo, Jennie Forsberg, Grace Hansen, John Hansen
Design Contributors: Dorothy Toth, Neil Klinepier

Library of Congress Control Number: 2017960496

Publisher's Cataloging in Publication Data

Names: Murray, Julie, author.
Title: Amphibians / by Julie Murray.
Description: Minneapolis, Minnesota : Abdo Zoom, 2019. | Series: Animal classes |
    Includes online resources and index.
Identifiers: ISBN 9781532122958 (lib.bdg.) | ISBN 9781532123931 (ebook) |
    ISBN 9781532124426 (Read-to-me ebook)
Subjects: LCSH: Amphibians--Juvenile literature. | Herpetology--Juvenile literature. |Speciation
    (Biology)--Juvenile literature. | Amphibians--Behavior--Juvenile literature.
Classification: DDC 597.81--dc23

Table of Contents

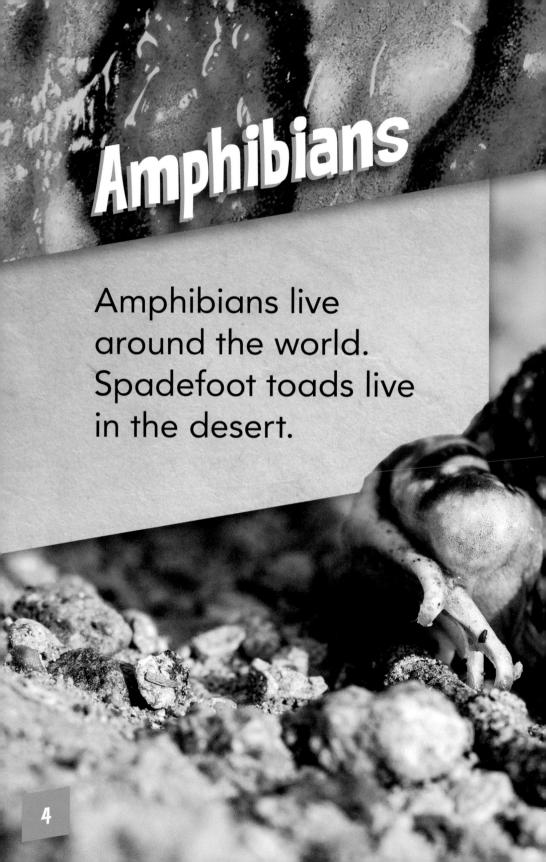

Amphibians

Amphibians live around the world. Spadefoot toads live in the desert.

There are more than 6,000 different **species**. What do they have in common?

Amphibians are
vertebrates.
Alpine newts have
small backbones.

Most have smooth, moist skin. A caecilian looks like a worm.

11

They are **cold-blooded**. A fire salamander sits in the sun. This keeps it warm.

They spend the first part
of their lives in water.

15

Amphibians lay eggs in water. Most frog eggs float. When they hatch, they are **tadpoles**!

Tadpoles have **gills** to breathe. They do not have legs yet.

Tadpoles grow legs and lungs. They can breathe air now.

They can live on land too!
Soon they will be adults.

Amphibian Traits

- Are **cold-blooded**
- Most have smooth and moist skin
- Lay soft, jellylike eggs
- Have a backbone
- Spend their early life in water
- Adults are **carnivores**

Glossary

carnivore – an animal that eats other animals.

cold-blooded – having a body temperature that varies with the environment.

gill – an organ used for breathing by amphibians and other animals that live in water.

species – a group of living things that look alike and can have babies together.

tadpole – a young frog or toad.

vertebrate – an animal that has a skeleton with a backbone inside its body.

Index

Online Resources

Booklinks
NONFICTION NETWORK
FREE! ONLINE NONFICTION RESOURCES

To learn more about amphibians, please visit **abdobooklinks.com**. These links are routinely monitored and updated to provide the most current information available.